Public Sector Competency-Based Development and Self-Assessment Handbook

Public Sector Competency-Based Development and Self-Assessment Handbook

A Self Assessment Handbook for Public Servants, Managers, Supervisors and Trainers

EMERSON. J. JONES

ISBN: Softcover   978-1-5434-9087-9
               eBook   978-1-5434-9086-2

Print information available on the last page.

Rev. date: 06/21/2018

To order additional copies of this book, contact:
Xlibris
800-056-3182
www.Xlibrispublishing.co.uk
Orders@Xlibrispublishing.co.uk
780621

People and Institutions

"An empowered organisation is one in which individuals have the knowledge, skill, desire and opportunity to personally succeed in a way that leads to organisational success"

Stephen R Covey

A handbook that identifies individual
competencies and Training Needs

Public Sector Competency - Based Development and Training with a strategic focus on:

- Enhancing governance, management and service delivery capacity of the public service
- Developing sustainable capacities of ministries, departments and non - ministerial institutions in a focused and consistent manner
- Achieving higher levels of performance effectiveness and efficiency
- Executing new and emergent Government mandates
- Enhancing capability of human resources
- Achieving improvements in public sector governance systems
- Providing linkages of training interventions to skills and competencies requirements
- Supporting the process of institution building and change management
- Contributing to the realisation of National Development Plans and Country's Vision
- Addressing urgent need for training and development at different levels of the public service
- Promoting development and training qualification outcomes and impacts
- Ensuring consistency with non – training development activities
- Responding to human resource "drivers" such as; career advancement, career planning, job redesign, service re – remodelling, change management, skill gaps and new technology

ABOUT THIS HANDBOOK

Welcome to this Public Sector Competency - Based Development and Self - Assessment Handbook. It is intended as an essential guide for use by those working mainly in the public and civil service, as well as, corporate governance sector. The competencies identified aim to support various professionally oriented training, such as, applied in-house tailored training, continuing professional development, specialist accredited training, examination based training, professional qualifications designed to suit graduates, fully qualified accountants and senior professionals so as to ensure requisite competencies are met among workers.

The handbook addresses the capacity and capability gaps of individuals and organisations at the pre-service, in-service and continuing professional development training systems respectively, by identifying the competencies and skills that are viewed as essential and where training interventions would need to be directed.

It focuses on a range of competencies, including job specific or functional competencies, essential competencies and common or generic competencies, which when acquired, allow the employee to perform a task or function at a specifically defined level of proficiency that will result in improved level of organisational and individual performance. This in turn will signpost all competency development and training needs at the basic, intermediate and advanced levels of knowledge, skills and abilities.

An important feature of the handbook is that it will enable individuals and their organisations to identify the competencies that are lacking and to address perceived factors, intrinsic and others that impede workers' performance. Hence the training contents at each level are intended to match the range of competencies that are deemed appropriate for the job and performance of employees and effective functioning of their organisations.

The handbook is written with a focus on achieving greater organisational impact and effectiveness, individual performance and efficiency, value adding and outcomes based learning.

CONTENTS

ACKNOWLEDGEMENTS

The author would like to express sincere thanks to many of his professional colleagues and particularly those involve in the public finance management and procurement disciplines who have contributed to this work. Their contributions were made through reviews, comments and suggestions, as well as, by reworking many of the sections produced.

There were a number of key individuals whose efforts in the design and re-modeling of sections are gratefully acknowledged. Many thanks to Fitzallan Regisford for the advice and insights which have been instrumental in the production of this book and to James Daniels for his technical guidance having agreed to review many of the initial training topics and objectives provided and to test the many thinking and definitions included.

Much of my thinking and decisions were shaped by the inputs of colleagues who have provided me with copies of various professional training reports. These were produced as part of the many international assignments undertaken by the team of which I was the leader.

To my daughters, Jennifer and Sonia who reviewed the many draft copies produced and for their support and encouragement throughout this journey my special thanks.

PREFACE

In order to optimise the value added by employees, public sector managers have a significant role to play in building the institutional, management and systemic capacity of departments and capabilities of their employees. They would need to define the competencies they have, those they need to sustain, and those that need to be grown. This is with respect to the full spectrum of roles, responsibilities and accountabilities that are commensurate with the levels of governance, leadership and management needed within their organisations. Institutions will have to clarify how these can be developed and monitored, as well as, how best to assess current capabilities, and what training and development interventions are necessary. They will also need to indicate what resources are required to further improve the organisation's ability to fulfill its mandate.

The public sector competency profiling framework is largely based on five essential criteria, namely, (i) that the public and civil service continues to be part of an evolving institutional and management culture, (ii) senior managers are required to steer, drive and anchor many reform, transformation, modernisation and continuous improvement efforts, (iii) the introduction of important management "drivers" such as, policy development and execution, sector policy outcomes and impacts, performance measures and targets and resource utilisation, (iv) building capacities for improved service delivery and (v) application of national, regional and international benchmarks on skills and competency development.

In this handbook is information which will enable the design of training programmes and courses that would enhance the leadership, governance, management and service delivery capacity of the public service. These are intended and to equip public servants to serve more efficiently and effectively for achieving desired policy outcomes and impacts.

It deals with a competency - based framework that provides for a structured approach which will enable managers and employees to identify and clarify training needs at the individual, job and organisational levels.

The use of this handbook is also intended to help control the proliferation of capacity development and training activities in public sector entities and ensure consistency with non-training support activities.

It will also enhance and further the professionalisation of the public service, and bring the level of performance to international standards.

1. INTRODUCTION

The development of this public sector competency - based and self - assessment handbook aims to solve the fundamental problem of skills and qualification gaps, namely, those individuals cannot define missing knowledge, skills and attributes when these are unknown to them. With the aim to enhance employees' competencies this handbook will help respondents identify their individual competency development and training needs. It also provides the basis for a comprehensive curriculum that is relevant and common to all government agencies regardless of the specialised or professional competencies in respective functional areas. More importantly it lays the foundation for the future capacity development and performance effectiveness of organisations within the public sector.

In the handbook reference is made to a hierarchy of competency models detailing the relative complexity of context and diversity of duties and tasks at different levels of employment. It targets five levels of competencies in the public sector including national and sub-national entities.

Within the public sector the following general target groups and related competencies can be identified: (i) Governance and Leadership Competencies for Director Generals, managing and executive directors and senior managers (or equivalent); (ii) Professional Staff Competencies, -- based on their profession e.g. accountants and auditors; (iii) Public Sector Management Competencies -- for middle and higher level managers, and executive officers managing a programme or common service, (iv) Programme and Project Management Competencies -- for programme and project officers and technical support staff and (v) Basic Office Competencies -- for operational and administrative staff.

The methodology used for defining public sector competencies refers to the context of public sector reform, transformation, modernisation

1

and continuous improvements involving new legislation, regulations, normative guidelines, standards and measures. The context of government work is further defined in terms of systemic reform, such as, assignment of new mandates, new delineation of responsibilities, new inter-agency relations and improved citizens' management. Furthermore government agencies are usually assigned new functional determinations and work areas that acquire new duties and tasks to accomplish and new performance standards to achieve.

At the individual level involving different categories of employees the needs are defined in packages of competencies which are required to meet new standards, perform new duties and tasks, and accomplish new functions of agencies. Other references to identify the package of competencies point to the following universal competency training areas:

- Providing strategic direction, and understanding the political context and wider environment
- Making effective decisions, reaching evidence based strategies, evaluating options, impacts, risks and solutions to maximize return while minimising risk and balancing a range of considerations to provide sustainable outcomes
- Effecting improvements and creating effective change
- Leading and communicating
- Building essential capabilities of staff
- Working collaboratively, partnering and engaging with people
- Achieving outcomes
- Managing a quality service
- Delivering value for money
- Dealing with new international concepts of Public Management and Democratic Governance, notably those concerning transparency and accountability

The handbook deals with the short and medium term interventions in training to enhance the human resource capabilities and support on - going capacity building to address long term reform initiatives and medium to long term systemic adjustments of mandates, structures, functions and tasks.

It is designed for use by human resource managers, head of training departments, lecturers and trainers, as well as, departmental managers, mainly for training needs assessment that will identify explicit gaps in knowledge and skills and their relevance to the job and performance of employees and their organisations

There is information that may be used for curriculum development and training delivery programmes and courses to enhance the governance, management and service delivery capacity, as well as, improve performance in the execution of new and emergent government mandates and to equip public servants to serve more effectively.

Finally this handbook has been created as a training resource to help managers plan, manage and achieve successful learning outcomes. It provides for an interactive and challenging application that will enable public officials find their learning experience productive, stimulating and rewarding. The aim is to provide trainees with the opportunity to establish a firm foundation for a successful career in the public and civil service.

2. TRAINING NEEDS ASSESSMENT (TNA)

This Training Needs Assessment is designed to gauge the need for training based on individually identified needs for those Spending Organisations (Ministries, Departments and Agencies) staff that directly involve the following disciplines.

Functional Areas and Disciplines

The Competency content is divided into eleven Functional Disciplines, namely:

1. **Accounting** - topics related to the recording, processing, and reporting of financial data.

2. **Audit** - topics related to risk management, internal and external audit, audit reporting and the process or responding to audit recommendations.

3. **Budget** - topics related to the development of plans, formulation and expenditure of appropriated funds. Most budget topics are directly or indirectly related to programme or performance budgeting methods, including capital budgeting

4. **Finance** - topics related to revenue, treasury operations, taxation, chart of accounts, fees, and cash management.

5. **Internal Audit** - to utilize the internal audit function to protect organisations from risks and the recommendations for improvements.

6. **IT, ICT, IFMIS** - topics related to Information Technology, Information and Communication Technology, and Integrated Financial Management Information Systems. This includes

issues related to hardware, software, establishment and use of systems.

7. **Leadership and Governance** - topics related to leading organisations, teams or projects, skills in delegation, use of parliamentary procedure and political processes, strategic planning, policy formulation and execution and leading and managing change.

8. **Management** - topics related to systems management, organisational operations, process flow, project management and administration.

9. **Planning, Monitoring and Evaluation** - topics related to the function of developing plans, and monitoring and evaluating, the overall implementation of policy, programmes and plans and policy impact evaluation

10. **Procurement** - topics related to the process of procuring goods and services, including the development of bid packages, evaluation criteria, taking possession of goods, storage, and disposal

11. **Professional Development** - topics related to participation in professional organisations, skills in proposal and report writing, and technical skills. Included are commercial skills and behaviours, delivering successful projects and programmes and redesigning services and delivering them digitally

3. TRAINING TOPICS, OBJECTIVES AND RELEVANCE TO WORK

This section of the book deals with topics covered in each of the functional disciplines to ensure that the appropriate content is offered to the appropriate level of government work and officials. The topics are divided into three levels.

1. **Basic** - the topics convey basic learning about the subject. These are appropriate for all levels of personnel with an interest to learn more about the topic. Substantial background materials on the subject are distributed. The level of the content is for Administrative Support and Technicians.

2. **Intermediate** - the topics are appropriate for mid-level managers with responsibilities related to the administration of projects, programmes, or activities related to the topic. Courses are highly interactive and concentrate on the issues/problems of the managers attending the programme. The level of the content is for Managers.

3. **Advanced** - the topics are directed at government officials responsible for making policy and high-level governance and management decisions related to the topic. Courses are highly interactive and may include individual consulting provided to the participants. The level of the content is for those in Leadership

    The training topics for each discipline are covered and the training objectives for each training topic in each discipline are stated.
    In this section the degree of relevance of training topics identified to the job of the post holder is set out. This is to be determined from analysis by the departmental manager or supervisor and employee concerned.

Lastly it makes mention as to whether the training of the employee is desired or not.

Hence this section defines the inter – relatedness of the training topics, training objectives, the relevance of the training topics to the work of the individual and whether the training is desired.

4. STEPS IN CONDUCTING COMPETENCY SELF - ASSESSMENT

The introduction of the Competency Self - Assessment Framework is intended to determine the capabilities needed to deliver high quality, value for money service to the public. It is a process that gives a cross - government view of the skill levels and requirements and a baseline for comparison.

The framework will be used for training and development discussions and for decisions about career progression. In this arrangement there are a number of areas that will need to be assessed. These include, training topics to be covered, training objectives to be achieved, the relevance of the employee work (including the roles, responsibilities and accountabilities) to the training.

In assessing training needs this will require the organisational and business objectives of ministries, departments and agencies to be clearly set out, and should include the goals, policies, roles and responsibilities. This will be followed by a performance gap analysis that would identify other factors, such as the lack of resource, or poor morale that may negatively impact employee performance and which cannot be solved by training alone.

This should next be followed by determining the target group or individuals to be trained.

1. ACCOUNTING

1.1 Basic - the courses convey basic learning about the subject. These are appropriate for all levels of personnel with an interest to learn more about the topic. Substantial background materials on the subject are distributed.

	TRAINING TOPIC	TRAINING OBJECTIVE	RELEVANCE TO WORK 4 – Very Relevant, mandatory for work 3 – Relevant, useful for work 2 – Partially Relevant, some relevance. 1 – Not Relevant, no relation to work				Training Desired	
			4	3	2	1	Yes	No
1	**Overview of the Government Accounting System**	To identify the basic features and principles of the Government Accounting system and apply the Uniform Guidelines and Procedures for Government Funds and Property. To be able to advocate that financial reports be utilized in the evaluation of the financial / budgetary aspect of an organisation.						
2	**The Electronic Government Accounting System**	To recognise and operate the basic features of the electronic government accounting system.						
3	**Uniform Guidelines and Procedures in Recording and Posting Financial Transactions**	To record financial transactions, and prepare and maintain General and Subsidiary Ledgers consistent with the Uniform Guidelines and Procedures prescribed.						
4	**Preparation of Financial Reports and Statements**	To prepare financial reports and statements which meet regular and special reporting requirements.						
5	**Updates on Policies and Guidelines Affecting Employees' Contributions to Social Security / Financial Institutions**	To be updated on and to apply existing and new policies and guidelines affecting employee benefits and contributions to Social Security / Financial Institutions in preparing the payroll and in processing the payment of employee benefits.						

6	**Overview of Internal Control Systems**	To identify the basic concepts, principles, tools and techniques in the installation, implementation, monitoring and evaluation of the internal controls, consistent with the National Guidelines on Internal Control Systems. To develop strategies to strengthen the Internal Control System on finances of an organization.						
7	**Manual Books Maintenance**	To ensure consistent practices in the maintenance of manual financial books.						
8	**Objectives of the Accounting System**	To describe the guidelines and procedures in accounting for government funds and property, coding structure, and accounting books, reports and forms.						
9	**Accrual Accounting under**	To use the modified accrual basis of accounting.						
10	**One Fund Concept**	To use the single fund account concept, and list the laws/situation when there may be variance.						

1.2 Intermediate - the courses are appropriate for mid-level managers with responsibilities related to the administration of projects, programs, or activities related to the topic. Courses are highly interactive and concentrate on the issues/problems of the managers attending the programme.

	TRAINING TOPIC	TRAINING OBJECTIVE	RELEVANCE TO WORK 4 – Very Relevant, mandatory for work 3 – Relevant, useful for work 2 – Partially Relevant, some relevance. 1 – Not Relevant, no relation to work				Training Desired	
			4	3	2	1	Yes	No
1	Overview of the Government Accounting System	To identify the basic features and principles of the Government Accounting system and apply the Uniform Guidelines and Procedures for Government Funds and Property. To identify financial reports necessary to facilitate determination of monthly available allotments, cash for possible utilization of savings / realignment / refocusing of projects / programs. To ensure accurate financial reports prepared by designated staff.						
2	Laws and Regulations on Government Expenditures	To identify and apply the various accounting and auditing rules and regulations governing disbursements of government funds, particularly those covering personal services, traveling expenses, procurement of supplies and materials, repairs and maintenance of motor vehicles and government facilities, capital outlay and other forms of expenditures.						
3	Financial Report / Statement Analysis	To verify and analyse financial information reflected in the Financial Reports / Statements and provide Management with accurate and reliable information as basis for policy and decision-making.						
4	Establishing and Operating Internal Control Systems	To apply the necessary concepts, principles, tools and techniques in the installation, implementation, monitoring and evaluation of the internal controls, consistent with the National Guidelines on Internal Control Systems.						
5	Verification and Reconciliation of Financial and Non-Financial Data	To verify propriety and completeness of transaction documentation and facilitate inter-office coordination for the reconciliation of financial and non-financial data.						

6	**Special Accounts in the General Fund**	To use special accounts in the General Fund and be able to complete and maintain subsidiary ledgers.								
7	**Chart of Accounts and Account**	To use the current and modified chart of accounts and coding system.								
8	**Books of Accounts: Journals**	To establish and maintain Journals: • CRJ, Cash Receipts Journal • CDJ, Cash Disbursements Journal • CKDJ, Check Disbursements Journal • GJ, General Journal								
9	**Books of Accounts: Ledgers**	To establish and maintain Ledgers, and Subsidiary Ledgers: • GL, General Ledger • Cash, Subsidiary Ledger • Receivables, Subsidiary Ledger • Inventories, Subsidiary Ledger • Investments, Subsidiary Ledger • Property, Plant and Equipment, Subsidiary Ledger • Liabilities, Subsidiary Ledger • Income, Subsidiary Ledger • Expenses, Subsidiary Ledger								
10	**Books of Accounts: Cashbooks and Reports**	To establish and maintain Accounts Cashbooks: • Cashbook – Cash in Treasury • Cashbook – Cash in Bank • Cashbook – Cash Advances • RCD, Report of Collections and Deposits (daily) • RAAF, Report of Accountability for Accountable Forms (monthly)								
11	**Preparation of Financial Statements**	To prepare, verify, and present Financial Statements, including: • Balance Sheet • Statement of Income and Expenses • Statement of Cash Flows • Trial Balance								
12	**Registries to Control Appropriations, Allotments, and Obligations**	To prepare, verify, and present registries, including: • RAAOCO, Registry of Appropriations, Allotments and Obligations – Capital Outlay • RAAOMO, Registry of Appropriations, Allotments and Obligations – Maintenance and Other Operating Expenses • RAAOPS, Registry of Appropriations, Allotments and Obligations – Personal Services • RAAOFE, Registry of Appropriations, Allotments and Obligations – Financial Expenses								

13	Maintenance of Financial Expenses	To maintain financial expenses (bank charges, interest, fees) separately from Maintenance and Other Operating Expenses.						
14	Perpetual Inventory of Supplies and Materials	To maintain a perpetual inventory system for supplies and materials, apart from items procured out of petty cash for immediate use.						
15	Valuation of Inventory	To assign cost of ending inventor of supplies and materials.						
16	Construction of Assets	To cost or capitalize assets under construction utilizing the current practices.						
17	Public Infrastructure	To prepare, verify, and present public infrastructure registries, including: RPIB, Registry of Public Infrastructure – Bridges RPIR, Registry of Public Infrastructure – Roads RPIP, Registry of Public Infrastructure – Plazas, Monuments, and others						
18	Depreciation, Calculation and Use	To calculate depreciation for all property, plant and equipment.						
19	Reclassification of Obsolete and Unserviceable Assets	To "write-off" those assets which are no longer of value.						
20	General Accounting Plan	To produce a General Accounting Plan specific to the Unit (graphic and verbal representation).						
21	Management Procedures for Budgetary Accounts	To identify all processes, responsible persons and steps related to Budgetary Account procedures, including: Appropriations, Allotments, and Obligations.						
22	Income Collections and Deposits	To maintain separate functions of the accountant and treasurer in the keeping of books and depository accounts.						
23	Maintenance of Income Accounts	To identify different types of income and code separately income sources, including: general income, specific income, real property, delinquencies, fines and penalties, borrowing, sale of property, and bonds.						
24	Reporting and Verification for Collections and Deposits	To issue receipts, and make closing Report of Collections and Deposits (RCD). To follow deposit process and regulations. To maintain accountable forms.						
25	Disbursement Certification and Approval	To describe/use the process to certify, approve, maintain supporting vouchers and payrolls, and the process to certify that funds are available.						

26	**Check Disbursement Process**	To describe and comply with procedures to make payments by check, recording, release, reporting and the disbursement process.						
27	**Payments in Cash**	To describe and comply with reporting, advances, use of petty cash, and the cash disbursement process.						
28	**Purchase or Construction of Property, Plant and Equipment**	To account for expenditures for all categories of capital purchases, and account for works in progress.						
29	**Disbursement Transactions Accounting Entries**	To debit and credit the correct accounting entries for every transaction involving disbursement of funds.						
30	**Overview of Accounting-Related IT Policies**	To know relevant policies, rules and regulations concerning accounting-related IT operations.						

1.3 Advanced - the courses are directed at government officials responsible for making policy and high-level management decisions related to the topic. Courses are highly interactive and may include individual consulting provided to the participants.

	TRAINING TOPIC	TRAINING OBJECTIVE	RELEVANCE TO WORK 4 – Very Relevant, mandatory for work 3 – Relevant, useful for work 2 – Partially Relevant, some relevance. 1 – Not Relevant, no relation to work				Training Desired	
			4	3	2	1	Yes	No
1	**Overview of the Government Accounting System**	To identify the basic features and principles of the Government Accounting system and apply the Uniform Guidelines and Procedures for Government Funds and Property.						
2	**Laws and Regulations on Government Expenditures**	To identify and apply the various accounting and auditing rules and regulations governing disbursements of government funds, particularly those covering personal services, traveling expenses, procurement of supplies and materials, repairs and maintenance of motor vehicles and government facilities, capital outlay and other forms of expenditures.						
3	**Financial Management for Public Managers**	To identify and apply the tools, techniques, practices and policies for putting into place structures and processes that will strengthen the elements of financial management and ensure the attainment of its objectives.						
4	**Interpreting Accounting Reports**	Using accounting data to make interpretations of the functioning of projects and programs.						
5	**Analysing the Budget**	Ensuring that budget marks accurately meet the needs of the submitting departments. Promoting the use of performance indicators.						
6	**Responding to the Budget**	Correspondence between policy makers, administrators, and departments related to initial and final budget marks.						
7	**Transactions in Error and Unique Occurrences**	To account for losses, errors in accounting and coding, and all unique transactions and suspensions, disallowances, and charges.						
8	**Adjusting and Closing Entries**	To make adjusting entries prior to the development of Balance Sheets, and Statements of Income and Expenses.						

9	**Preparation and use of the Trial Balance**	To describe and use the procedures required to prepare the Trial Balance, and to utilize for policy decision making.						
10	**Fund Accounting**	To make accounting entries used for special funds, trust funds, and donor funds, and to utilise fund data for policy decision making.						

2. AUDIT

2.1 Basic - the courses convey basic learning about the subject. The course is appropriate for all levels of personnel with an interest to learn more about the topic. Substantial background materials on the subject are distributed.

	TRAINING TOPIC	TRAINING OBJECTIVE	RELEVANCE TO WORK 4 – Very Relevant, mandatory for work 3 – Relevant, useful for work 2 – Partially Relevant, some relevance. 1 – Not Relevant, no relation to work				Training Desired	
			4	3	2	1	Yes	No
1	**Risk Analysis as a Basis for Audit**	To understand the definition of risk, risk analysis, and how identification of risks contributes to the basic format of auditing.						
2	**Overview of Auditing**	To define auditing, distinction between auditing and accounting, types of audits, types of auditors, government auditing, and the functions of the Supreme Audit Institution.						
3	**Audit Planning**	To gather initial evaluation information, establishing audit objectives and scope, audit materiality, audit risk, establishing an audit program, and internal control systems.						
4	**Audit Execution**	To us audit evidence and methods, types of audit tests (systems based, direct substantive).						
5	**Audit Reporting**	To prepare for the exit conference, draft and final reports, supervision and review.						
6	**Follow Up Audit Report**	To follow-up an audit report.						
7	**Audit Opinions**	To understand the meaning of unqualified, qualified, adverse, and disclaimer opinions.						
8	**The Internal Audit**	To utilize the internal audit function to protect organizations from risks and the develop recommendations for improvements.						
9	**The External Audit**	To utilize the process of external audits for financial, compliance, performance and other types of audits.						

10	**Government Audit**	To understand how government audits its own branches, ministries, or units, for use of both government funds and externally provided funds.						
11	**Audit Report**	To develop the audit report, development of findings and recommendations.						

2.2 Intermediate - the courses are appropriate for mid-level managers with responsibilities related to the administration of projects, programs, or activities related to the topic. Courses are highly interactive and concentrate on the issues/problems of the managers attending the program.

	TRAINING TOPIC	TRAINING OBJECTIVE	RELEVANCE TO WORK 4 – Very Relevant, mandatory for work 3 – Relevant, useful for work 2 – Partially Relevant, some relevance. 1 – Not Relevant, no relation to work				Training Desired	
			4	3	2	1	Yes	No
1	**Financial Statement Audit**	To examine financial statements to determine if they fairly present the results of operations as well as cash flow.						
2	**Performance Audit**	To use a performance audit to determine the effectiveness, efficiency and economy of a project, program, or institution.						
3	**Compliance Audit**	To use a compliance audit to determine if rules, policies, laws or regulations are being implemented.						
4	**The Government Audit for Good Governance**	To understand how government auditing promotes good governance, good practices, and capacity development.						
5	**Audit Evidence**	To understand how to assess and obtain evidence which is competent, relevant, and reasonable. Usage of sources and types of evidence.						
6	**Audit Methods and Tests**	To use methods of collecting evidence and the test of controls, test of details. Types and usage of sampling methods.						

2.3 Advanced - the courses are directed at local government officials responsible for making policy and high-level management decisions related to the topic. Courses are highly interactive and may include individual consulting provided to the participants.

	TRAINING TOPIC	TRAINING OBJECTIVE	RELEVANCE TO WORK 4 – Very Relevant, mandatory for work 3 – Relevant, useful for work 2 – Partially Relevant, some relevance. 1 – Not Relevant, no relation to work				Training Desired	
			4	3	2	1	Yes	No
1	**Audit Plan Development**	To develop the Audit Plan, development of a plan for utilising both internal and external audits.						
2	**International Audit Organizations**	To understand the standards and roles of international auditing organisations.						
3	**The Role of the Commission on Audit**	To understand and utilize the assistance of the Commission on Audit. Government obligations to work with and adhere to findings.						
4	**The Role of Auditing in the Relationship Between the Legislative and Administrative Bodies**	To understand that the legislative bodies and administrative bodies have their own need and requirements to use audits to ensure compliance. Both levels of institutions use audits to determine the proper management.						
5	**Development and Implementation of an Audit Program**	To utilise an audit programme as a portion of an overall management, monitoring, and evaluation tool. Aspects include: establishing controls, risk assessment, control activities, Information and communications, monitoring, and overall capacity development for the organization.						
6	**Minimising Fraud Risks**	To minimise fraud, set expectations, motivate performance, and develop attitudes and behaviors opposed to potential fraud and corruption.						
7	**Fraud Red Flags**	To detect danger signals of fraud.						
8	**Responding to Audit Reports**	To develop a plan to address audit recommendations or challenge audit findings. Implementing the plan in preparation for an audit follow-up.						
9	**Orientation on the National Guidelines on Internal Control System**	To gain awareness of the National Guidelines on Internal Control System.						

3. BUDGET

3.1 Basic - the courses convey basic learning about the subject. The course is appropriate for all levels of personnel with an interest to learn more about the topic. Substantial background materials on the subject are distributed.

	TRAINING TOPIC	TRAINING OBJECTIVE	RELEVANCE TO WORK 4 – Very Relevant, mandatory for work 3 – Relevant, useful for work 2 – Partially Relevant, some relevance. 1 – Not Relevant, no relation to work				Training Desired	
			4	3	2	1	Yes	No
1	**Why and How Organisations use Budgets**	To describe the various budgeting implementation strategies organisations use.						
2	**Understanding of the Budget Guideline (Budget Line and Code)**	To understand the budget guideline with the code numbers.						
3	**Linking Accounting to the Budget**	To be able to record the transaction with the correct codes, and relate the accounting codes to the budget categories.						
4	**Budget Reporting**	To be able to report expenditures and relate them to the budget categories.						
5	**Budget Reporting to Donors**	To be able to report expenditures in terms and conditions which match donor formats.						
6	**Budget Control**	To be able to control expenditures according to budgeted amounts.						
7	**Budget Analysis**	To establish policies and procedures to trace budget variances.						
8	**Professional Financial Reports**	To produce financial reports which meet professional standards.						
9	**Budget Process**	To implement the budget process, and examples of best practices in budget process.						
10	**Participative Budgeting**	To identify the benefits, establish and utilize participative methods in the development of the budget.						
11	**Plan-Budget Linkage**	To develop and implement synchronized approaches to the development of annual budgets and annual plans.						

12	**Annual Investment Program Preparation**	To understand, develop, and implement and Annual Investment Program in simultaneous preparation and execution of the Budget.						
13	**The Program, Project, and Activities Structure**	To formulate and write: a logical framework, identification of Programs, Projects, and Activities, and determination of Performance Indicators.						

3.2 Intermediate - the courses are appropriate for mid-level managers with responsibilities related to the administration of projects, programs, or activities related to the topic. Courses are highly interactive and concentrate on the issues/problems of the managers attending the program.

	TRAINING TOPIC	TRAINING OBJECTIVE	RELEVANCE TO WORK 4 – Very Relevant, mandatory for work 3 – Relevant, useful for work 2 – Partially Relevant, some relevance. 1 – Not Relevant, no relation to work				Training Desired	
			4	3	2	1	Yes	No
1	Building the Budget from the Bottom-Up	To solicit from line departments their resource needs for implementation of the Annual Budget Plan.						
2	Assessing the Available Resources	To improve the effectiveness of financial forecasting.						
3	Establishment of the Budget Calendar	To utilize a Budget Calendar which provides guidance on budget planning for all Department staff.						
4	Budget Preparation Responsibilities	To delegate responsibilities for the preparation of the budget within each Department and improve the effectiveness of budgeting process.						
5	The Annual Plan and the Annual Budget	To Budgeting the linkages between the budgeting and planning cycles closer together. Eventually the Budget and the Planning Process will become one process resulting in the Program Budget.						
6	Budget Categories and Chart of Accounts	To ensure that budget preparations can be reflected in the Chart of Accounts.						
7	Integration of Donor Projects into Programs	To ensure that "off-book" projects are not conducted utilizing donor funding.						
8	Multi-Year Budget Planning and Budget Preparation	To adopt a 3 year MTBF/MTEF planning cycle of budget preparation.						
9	Capital Budgeting Cycle	To Bring the Capital Budgeting into synch with the Annual Budget and Annual Planning process.						
10	Performance Indicators	To developing performance indicators to measure both the quantity of work performed and the quality of work performed.						
11	Linkages Between Planning and Finance	To use financial data, expected revenue, and initial budget levels for use in the budget planning cycle.						

12	**Program and Performance Based Budgeting**	To develop program and performance based budgets, budget categories, authority to expend funds, and performance indicators.							
13	**Budget Monitoring**	To establish mechanisms to monitor the implementation of the budget. Ensure that expenditures occur in a timely manner to meet program objectives.							
14	**Budget Evaluation**	To establish a budget evaluation process which focuses on both implementation procedures and attainment of performance measures.							
15	**Budget Reporting**	To prepare and use budget reporting procedures. Developing the format and timeline for delivery of budget reports.							
16	**Capital Budget Development**	To use the public investment process to develop and implement the capital budget.							
17	**Coordination of Planning and Budget**	To develop methods of coordinating the roles of planning departments and budget departments.							
18	**Cost Accounting Procedures**	To use cost accounting procedures in the development of budgets.							
19	**Project Risk Checklist**	To use project risk checklists in the preparation of budgets and decision makers.							
20	**Project Manager Duties**	To describe the assignment of project managers to guide the development of all steps of budget and implementation process.							
21	**Budget Preparation Phase**	To prepare and implement the; budget call, prepare and submit budget proposals, conduct a budget hearing, prepare the local expenditure program, and prepare the budget message and budget of expenditures and sources of financing.							
22	**Budget of Expenditures and Sources of Financing**	To locate information and complete: • Summary Statement of Receipts and Expenditures • Estimated Expenditures by Program, Project, Activity, and by Sector • Actual and Estimated Expenditure Program • Staffing Summary							
23	**Budget of Expenditures and Sources of Financing**	To locate information and complete: • Summary Statement of Statutory and Contractual Obligations and Budgetary Requirements • Summary Statement of Long-Term Obligations and Indebtedness							
24	**Budget Preparation, 1**	To locate information and complete: • Statement of Receipts • Statement of Receipts and Expenditures							

25	**Budget Preparation, 2**	To locate information and complete: • Programmed Appropriation and Obligation by Object of Expenditure • Consolidated Programmed Appropriation and Obligation by Object of Expenditure • Personnel Schedule • Functional Statements, Objects and Expected results • Organizational Structure						
26	**Budget Preparation, 3**	To locate information and complete: • Statement of Debt Service • Statement of Statutory and Contractual Obligations and Budgetary Requirements						
27	**Budget Preparation, 4**	To locate information and complete: • Statement of Fund Operation • Statement o Funding Sources • Statement of Supplemental Appropriation						
28	**Budget Preparation, 5**	To locate information and complete BP Forms: • Special Provisions/Operating Policies						
29	**Technical Notes on Budget Preparation**	To utilize statistical and mathematical skills to prepare budget entries, comparisons, and develop trend tables.						
30	**Effectiveness of Budgets**	To utilize the requirements to put into practice the appropriation ordinance.						
31	**Budget Review**	To determine whether the budget ordinance complies with the requirements and limitations of the Government Code.						
32	**The Steps in the Budget Review Phase**	To construct and utilize a Budget Review Flow Chart.						
33	**Budget Review Forms**	To locate information and complete budget review Forms: • Checklist on Documentary and Signature Requirements for the Annual Budget • Checklist on Documentary and Signature Requirements for the Supplemental Budget • Table Recapitulating the Findings and Possible Review Actions						
34	**Budget Execution Phase**	To describe and utilize the main components of the Budget Execution Phase, including: legal basis, key players, budget execution flow chart, accounts in budget execution.						

35	**Steps in the Budget Execution Phase**	To describe and utilize the steps in the Budget Execution Phase, including: recording the approved appropriations, release of allotments, and preparing the cash program, summary of financial and physical performance targets, revise the Project Procurement Management Plan (PPMP), and Annual Procurement Plan (APP).						
36	**Implementing the Budget Execution Phase**	To describe and implement the Budget Execution Phase, including: obligate and disburse funds, adjust cash program for shortages and overages, provide corrective actions.						
37	**Budget Execution**	To locate information and complete: • Budget Matrix • Allotment Release Order • Summary of Financial and Physical Performance Targets • Detailed Financial and Physical Performance targets						
38	**Budget Accountability) Forms**	To locate information and complete: • Quarterly Report of Income • Quarterly Financial Report of Operations • Quarterly Physical Report of Operations • Statement of Receipts and Expenditures						
39	**Budget Performance Evaluation**	To locate information and complete: • Physical Performance Evaluation Form • Financial Performance Evaluation Form • Office/Department Performance Evaluation (to intermediate)						
40	**Cost Benefit Analysis Tools & Techniques**	To identify and apply cost-benefit analysis tools and techniques in prioritizing expenditures.						
41	**Establishment and Maintenance of Economic Enterprises**	To learn and understand the procedures and techniques in establishing economic enterprises, including preparation of project studies / feasibility studies on.						

3.3 Advanced - the courses are directed at local government officials responsible for making policy and high-level management decisions related to the topic. Courses are highly interactive and may include individual consulting provided to the participants.

	TRAINING TOPIC	TRAINING OBJECTIVE	RELEVANCE TO WORK 4 – Very Relevant, mandatory for work 3 – Relevant, useful for work 2 – Partially Relevant, some relevance. 1 – Not Relevant, no relation to work				Training Desired	
			4	3	2	1	Yes	No
1	**Effective Budget Delegation**	To delegate budget preparation and expenditure to the lowest possible level of government, while maintaining appropriate levels of authority, responsibility, and accountability.						
2	**Option Identification for Budget Purposes**	To develop different scenarios in the development of budgets, provision of alternative spending/achieving levels. How to modify budgets through decreases and increases.						
3	**Specifying Target Results**	To develop budget goals, and objectives, and relating performance indicators to achieving results.						
4	**Learning Lessons from Budget Implementation**	To use of the budget review process, institutionalizing planning steps which build on previous budget year and current year experiences.						
5	**Linking Recurrent and Capital Budgets**	To develop both Annual Operating (recurrent) and Capital budgets on the same time frame, methods of identifying recurrent costs related to capital expenditures.						
6	**Looking for Budget Efficiency Savings**	To develop programs which reward budget efficiency while maintaining programme effectiveness.						
7	**Cost Analysis**	To develop procedures to analyze costs, including the use of standard costing sheets and comparative studies.						
8	**Prioritization**	To balance the administrative needs with policy objectives to ensure that policy priority receive budgetary priority.						
9	**Analyzing Variations in Service Results**	To conduct comparative studies and results of service delivery in different units of government.						

10	Effective Consultation on Budgets	To use consultation with a wide variety of stake holders on the development and implementation of budgets. How to arrange and conduct consultative meetings and events, including public budget hearings.						
11	The Budget Presentation	To preparation the budget into a formal "presentation" (the final document) which conveys the intention of the budget to a large audience of the public.						
12	Capital Investment Planning	To move form funding of projects to funding of Programs. This is a means of moving from "individual project" thinking, to long-term "program" planning for capital investment.						
13	Transparent and Public Processes	To hold public meetings, and maintain on-going public reporting on the use of the budget.						
14	Operating and Maintenance Costs	To budget for operating and maintenance costs of capital projects (and departmental operation).						
15	Preparing Multi-Year Budget	To understand and use a multi-year budget, overlapping budget cycles, and the functions of reviewing, implementing, planning, estimating, and forecasting.						
16	The Budget Message	To develop the (draft) budget message for inclusion into the budget.						
17	Budget Authorization	To understand, draft, and utilize the enactment of the Appropriation Ordinance, including the involvement of mandatory participation/signatures and adherence to the flow chart.						
18	Changes in the Annual Budget: Supplemental Budget	To understand, draft, and introduce as an ordinance all supplemental authorized budget items.						
19	Budget Authorisation	To locate information and complete BA Forms: • Checklist on Documentary and Signature Requirements for the Annual Budget • Checklist on Documentary and Signature Requirements for the Supplemental Budget • Proposed New Appropriations Language • Program Appropriations and Obligation by Object • Approval Letter of the Executive • Veto Message Format Ordinance Authorizing Use of Savings and Augmentation.						

20	**Budget Accountability**	To describe and utilize the main components of the Budget Accountability Phase, including: legal basis, key players, budget accountability flow chart, and account for the budget execution.						
21	**Monitoring Budget Implementation**	To locate information and fulfill the monitoring function related to: appropriations, allotments, obligations, physical outputs and accomplishments, evaluation of each department/office, and review/evaluation of performance.						
22	**Sample Formats of Review Letters and Resolutions Related to the Budget Review**	To write and utilize notification letters as indicated by the current situation: • Declaring the Appropriation Ordinance Operative in its Entirety • Declaring the Appropriation Ordinance Operative in its Entirety Subject to Some Conditions • Declaring the Appropriation Ordinance Inoperative in its Entirety • Declaring the Appropriation Ordinance Inoperative in Part						
23	**Using Budget Performance Evaluation in Policy Formation**	To make decisions, modify, and implement improvements based on a Budget Performance Evaluation.						

4. FINANCE AND REVENUE ADMINISTRATION

4.1 Basic - the courses convey basic learning about the subject. The course is appropriate for all levels of personnel with an interest to learn more about the topic. Substantial background materials on the subject are distributed.

	TRAINING TOPIC	TRAINING OBJECTIVE	RELEVANCE TO WORK 4 – Very Relevant, mandatory for work 3 – Relevant, useful for work 2 – Partially Relevant, some relevance. 1 – Not Relevant, no relation to work				Training Desired	
			4	3	2	1	Yes	No
1	**Local Government Taxation**	To understand the fundamental principles of local government taxation, identify the scope of taxing powers, procedures for the collection of taxes and civil remedies for the collection of revenues.						
2	**Cash Management and Control**	To understand and apply the existing rules and regulations on the handling and custody of government funds, and to learn and institute the related controls to ensure proper safekeeping and disbursements of funds.						
3	**Anti-Corruption Laws and Measures**	To appreciate the need to (1) adopt and observe a Code of Ethics; (2) institute disciplinary rules and proceedings against erring officials; and (3) encourage vigilance among the staff and clientele. To be aware of existing anti-graft and corruption laws, rules and regulations.						
4	**Preparing the Statement of Receipts and Expenditure and Related Reports**	To be able to (1) Prepare the Statement of Receipts and Expenditures applying the common classification of accounts, using terminologies and timing of recording financial transactions in harmony in conformity with the IFRS; and (2) Identify the various source documents to be used in the preparation of reports and guidelines for the completion of the various report forms.						
5	**Local Government Revenue Administration**	To define local government revenue administration, identify its components, functions, structure and organization.						

4.2 Intermediate - the courses are appropriate for managers with responsibilities related to the administration of a department or projects, programmes, or activities related to the topic. Courses are highly interactive and concentrate on the issues/problems of the managers attending the programme.

TRAINING TOPIC	TRAINING OBJECTIVE	RELEVANCE TO WORK 4 – Very Relevant, mandatory for work 3 – Relevant, useful for work 2 – Partially Relevant, some relevance. 1 – Not Relevant, no relation to work				Training Desired	
		4	3	2	1	Yes	No
1 **Spending Organisation Sources of Revenue**	To identify the traditional and non-traditional sources of revenue and expand Spending Organization sources of revenues by exploring non-traditional revenue generation measures such as public-private partnerships (Joint Ventures & Build-Operate-Transfer Schemes) and bond flotation, among others.						
2 **Strategic Planning and Risk Management in Revenue Administration**	To develop skills in: (1) formulating vision and mission statements; (2) internal and external scanning; (3) compliance risk management; (4) resource allocation and prioritization; (5) budget-plan preparation, implementation and monitoring; and (6) performance evaluation.						
3 **Revenue Administration Diagnostics**	To understand the Conceptual Framework for Detailed Diagnostics of Local Government Revenue Administration and conduct the evaluation of the current revenue administration as basis for reforms.						
4 **Financial Reports Analysis and Verification**	To be familiar with the guidelines on verifying the accuracy of information in the financial reports, particularly in the Statement of Receipts and Expenditures and related reports; To develop aptitude in reconciling and ensuring the accuracy of information in the Reports; and To use the SRE as input in the determination of the Spending Organization's revenue forecasting and credit worthiness rating, among others.						
5 **Tax Audit Planning**	To define and understand tax audit, recognize the value of tax audit planning, identify the factors which should be considered in tax audit planning, learn how to develop audit plans (strategic, operational and case plans), and how to evaluate these plans.						

6	Taxpayer Audit Methods	To identify and understand the direct and indirect methods of taxpayer audits, formulate techniques for detecting non-filers, stop-filers and payment defaulters.						
7	Internal Controls in Local Government Revenue Administration	To identify and understand the basic concepts and elements of internal control and utilize tools and techniques in techniques in the installation, implementation, monitoring and evaluation of the internal controls in revenue administration consistent with the National Guidelines on Internal Control Systems.						
8	Cash Flow Programming and Management	(1) To be able to prepare a Cash Program taking into consideration the approved budget, and the financial and physical targets; and (2) To manage cash flows to ensure availability of cash for projects and activities and optimize cash balances.						
9	Debt Strategy	To develop a Debt strategy based on minimizing the cost of funding, reducing volatility in principal and interest payments, maintaining liquidity, improving the local government's creditworthiness rating, and increasing transparency.						
10	Enhancing Real Property Tax Administration	To identify strategies for enhancing Real Property Tax administration.						
11	Establishment and Updating of Spending Organisation Revenue Code	To identify and apply guidelines in the establishment and updating of Spending Organization Revenue Code.						
12	Tools and techniques in Tax Mapping	To identify and apply tools and techniques in tax mapping.						

4.3 Advanced - the courses are directed at senior level officials responsible for making policy decisions related to the topic. Courses are highly interactive and may include individual consulting provided to the participants.

	TRAINING TOPIC	TRAINING OBJECTIVE	RELEVANCE TO WORK 4 – Very Relevant, mandatory for work 3 – Relevant, useful for work 2 – Partially Relevant, some relevance. 1 – Not Relevant, no relation to work				Training Desired	
			4	3	2	1	Yes	No
1	**Revenue Policy Development**	To develop policy support for revenue administration reforms identified after evaluation, conduct public hearings and obtain legislative support and approval.						
2	**Debt Management**	To develop debt management policies, using as benchmarks policies used by other Spending Organization as well as national and international policies. Involvement of legislative bodies in the development of policy.						
3	**Revenue Administration Organisation and Structure**	To review the existing revenue administration organizational structure, be familiar with revenue organizational models, develop an Spending Organization-suited organizational structure and provide policy support to the restructuring of the revenue administration department/s.						
4	**Local Fiscal Capacity and Revenue Forecasting**	To determine local fiscal capacity and forecast revenues using the information in the financial reports, particularly in the Statement of Receipts and Expenditures and related reports. To develop policy for increasing fiscal capacity and strengthening revenue forecasting.						
5	**Taxpayer Incentive and Penalty System**	To develop policy for granting taxpayer incentives for compliance and imposition of stiffer penalties for non-compliance.						

5. INTERNAL AUDIT

5.1 Basic - the courses convey basic learning about the subject. The course is appropriate for all levels of personnel with an interest to learn more about the topic. Substantial background materials on the subject are distributed.

TRAINING TOPIC		TRAINING OBJECTIVE	RELEVANCE TO WORK 4 – Very Relevant, mandatory for work 3 – Relevant, useful for work 2 – Partially Relevant, some relevance. 1 – Not Relevant, no relation to work				Training Desired	
			4	3	2	1	Yes	No
1	**Overview of Internal Auditing**	To describe the role of internal audit, the relationship in the Spending Organization with other departments, and interaction with the administrative management and policy leadership of the Spending Organization.						
2	**Overview of Government Accounts and Audits**	To describe how government audits its branches, departments, Spending Organization, for use of both government funds and externally provided funds.						
3	**Risks Based Auditing**	To describe the importance of adopting a risk-based approach, the internal audit process, and stages of risk-based internal audit process.						
4	**Internal Audit Expectations**	To list and communicate the objectives, processes, and expectations of Internal Auditing, and agree on documentation, planning, activities, and timing of Internal Audits.						
5	**Understanding the Auditees**	To understand and list the audites' financial and operating processes and performance to determine the relevant processes for auditing.						
6	**Risk Analysis and Assessment**	To establish the key points of measurement, assessment, and potential risk the Internal Audit will address.						
7	**Developing the Internal Audit Plan**	To plan the Internal Audit activities and functions over a year's period.						
8	**Conducting the Internal Audit – The Ongoing Process**	To outline the process to be use for gathering information and process mapping, assessing process risks, assessing process performance and control gaps, and audit testing to validate process controls compliance.						

9	Communicating Internal Audit Findings and Recommendations	To summarizing audit results, statements of weaknesses and recommendations, and to draft reporting and findings letters.						
10	Promoting the Implementation of Internal Audit Recommendations	To maintaining a register of recommendations, and follow up on audit reports.						
11	Audit Documentation	To develop and utilize templates for Internal Audit.						
	Internal Audit Reporting Chain	To describe the reporting responsibilities of the Internal Audit Department; to the committees of the Sanguine.						
13	Review and Appraisal of Financial and Operating Controls	To review and appraise the soundness and application of accounting, financial and other controls, and physical accounting and safeguarding of Spending Organization assets against loss, fraud, embezzlement, or errors.						
14	Quality of Performance and Compliance with Policies, Plans and Procedures	To assess the compliance with Spending Organization policies, plans and procedures. Assess the quality of performance in implementing assignments and projects. Identification of errors in compliance and errors in the governing policies.						
15	The Verification Process	To verify the entries in source documents are correct, verify source documents are reflected in reports. To verify that entries are posted in the appropriate account, costs are apportioned, codes are correctly used, that cash counts are accurate, and receipts and daily registers are maintained.						
16	Proof of Bank Reconciliation	To verify that cash balances in accounts are accurately prepared by accounting/treasury.						
17	Proof of Accounts Receivable	To verify that the list of debtors is accurate and that rates, rents, fees, taxes, and penalties are correctly calculated.						
18	Confirmation of Inventories	To take a physical stock count, and verify record cards and ledgers.						
19	Insurance and Protection of Assets	To verify that assets are covered by insurance, are under guard, and that accurate lists of assets and their values are maintained.						
20	Depreciation and Valuation of Assets	To verify the value of assets through comparison of acquisition, payments, and book values. Ensure that depreciation rates are accurately applied.						
21	Verification of Bank Reserves, Investments, and Deposits	To verify deposits, the sources of credits, interest rates, and to verify liabilities.						

22	**Verification of Credit and Debt Management**	To verify that terms of credit are correct, and followed, and that liability lists are current.						
23	**Evaluation of Internal Controls**	To determine whether procedures in recording transactions are effective, use of manual and electronic systems, adequacy of personnel, and methods of retaining records.						
24	**Evaluation of performance and the PFM operating departments.**	To evaluate the plan of each PFM unit, work flow procedures, polices, achievement of objectives and individual performance.						
25	**Evaluation of Compliance**	To evaluate and ensure that policies, systems, laws, and recommendations are implemented.						
26	**Sophisticated Estimation Risks (Risk Based Audit (RBA) Risk Control Standards Matrix)**	To determine the accuracy, completeness, authorization, timelines and operation of: Journal Entries, Methods and Computations, Key Assumptions, Supporting Data and Information, Capture Operation Events and Facts.						
27	**Critical Information Processing Risks(Risk Based Audit (RBA) Risk Control Standards Matrix)**	To determine the accuracy, completeness, authorisation, timelines and operation of: Outputs and Journal Entries, Conversion/ Processing, Data Transfer, Data Input and Changes, Capture Operation Transactions.						
28	**Financial Report Processing Risks (Risk Based Audit (RBA) Risk Control Standards Matrix)**	To determine the accuracy, completeness, authorization, timelines and operation of: Statement and Disclosure Preparation, Principal Reporting Adjustments, Consolidation.						

5.2 Intermediate - the courses are appropriate for mid-level managers with responsibilities related to the administration of projects, programs, or activities related to the topic. Courses are highly interactive and concentrate on the issues/problems of the managers attending the program.

	TRAINING TOPIC	TRAINING OBJECTIVE	RELEVANCE TO WORK 4 – Very Relevant, mandatory for work 3 – Relevant, useful for work 2 – Partially Relevant, some relevance. 1 – Not Relevant, no relation to work				Training Desired	
			4	3	2	1	Yes	No
1	Internal Audit, Transparency, and Good Governance	To describe how internal auditing promotes transparency, good governance, and provides indicators for capacity development.						
2	Structuring Templates, Indicators, and Internal-Audit Tests	To develop and utilize both mandatory and special designed audit tools. Ensuring that internal audit measures contribute to the preparation for external audits.						
3	Maintaining Records an Working Papers	To develop and utilize security procedures to ensure that records and working papers are maintained safely.						
4	Audit Techniques	To utilize methods of documenting financial and operational processes, internal controls, audit testing, computer assisted audit techniques, Types and us of sampling methods.						
5	Performance Audit and "Value for Money" Recommendations	To use the performance audit to determine the effectiveness, efficiency and economy of a program, project, activity, or unit.						
6	Minimizing Fraud Risks	To detect danger signals of fraud, methods to minimize fraud, setting expectations to motivate performance, developing attitudes and behaviors opposed to potential fraud and corruption.						
7	Maintaining Internal Audit Check-Lists	To design and maintain checklists of internal audit against which all departments and units can measure the expectations and their performance over time.						

5.3 Advanced - the courses are directed at local government officials responsible for making policy and high-level management decisions related to the topic. Courses are highly interactive and may include individual consulting provided to the participants.

	TRAINING TOPIC	TRAINING OBJECTIVE	RELEVANCE TO WORK 4 – Very Relevant, mandatory for work 3 – Relevant, useful for work 2 – Partially Relevant, some relevance. 1 – Not Relevant, no relation to work				Training Desired	
			4	3	2	1	Yes	No
1	**Internal Audit Organisation**	To understand and reinforce the roles.						
2	**Structuring Templates, Indicators, and Internal-Audit Tests**	To develop and utilize both mandatory and special designed audit tools. Ensuring that internal audit measures contribute to the preparation for external audits.						
3	**Management Initiated Reform of an Internal Audit Unit**	To promote the function of internal audit, define the organizational structure and reporting, staff recruitment and introducing the changes required to comply and improve internal audit ratings.						
4	**Strategic Audit Plan Development**	To assist in the development and implementation of the Strategic Audit Plan.						
5	**Internal-Audit Report Interpretation**	To interpret the meaning of the Internal-Audit report, evaluation of performance, procedures, and assessing stakeholders' satisfaction/ response.						
6	**Internal Audit Quality Management Assurance and Improvement**	To implement internal quality management and assurance systems within the Internal Audit department.						
7	**Managing Internal Audit and External Audit Relationships**	To promote management awareness of the nature, role, scope and benefits of Internal Auditing and improving coordination between Internal and External audit agencies.						
8	**Future Challenges of Internal Audit**	To maintain a focus on promoting a risk-based Internal Audit system, enhancing the role of the Internal Auditor, and independence and reporting responsibilities.						
9	**Measurement of Liquidity, Ability to Meet Short-Term Liabilities**	To calculate the liquidity rate of the Spending Organization based on the revenues and obligations, and conduct a risk assessment related to late/ non-reporting.						

10	Increase in Local Income	To measure the income from all sources, and conduct a risk assessment of financial statements due to incomplete recording of income.							
11	Fund Management	To measure if the Spending Organization is spending within the budget limit and that allotments are efficiently utilized, and conduct a risk assessment related to meeting program priorities.							
12	Financial Leverage, Ability to Meet Long-Term Obligations	To measure the ability of the Spending Organization to settle all obligations as they fall due, and conduct a risk assessment related to potential collection suits, fees, and credit rating.							
13	Performance Review Summary	To summarize the performance of revenue, asset, and expense accounts, and analysis of the Report of Revenue and Receipts (of current and prior years), Reports of Collections & Deposits, Statement of Cash Flows, Balance Sheet, Statement of Income and Expenses, Report of Disbursements and Report of Checks Issued, and Status of Appropriation, Allotment and Obligations.							

6. IT / ICT / IFMIS

6.1 Basic - the courses convey basic learning about the subject. Courses are appropriate for all levels of personnel with an interest to learn more about the topic. Substantial background materials on the subject are distributed.

	TRAINING TOPIC	TRAINING OBJECTIVE	RELEVANCE TO WORK 4 – Very Relevant, mandatory for work 3 – Relevant, useful for work 2 – Partially Relevant, some relevance. 1 – Not Relevant, no relation to work				Training Desired	
			4	3	2	1	Yes	No
1	**Basic Office Applications**	To learn and utilize basic Microsoft Office Applications (Word, Excel, Access, PowerPoint etc.)						
2	**Basic Computer (Hardware) Operation, Maintenance and Troubleshooting**	To learn how to operate and maintain computer hardware and to acquire basic troubleshooting skills.						
3	**Integrated Financial Management Information System (IFMIS)**	To define IFMIS, identify its objectives, its scope and coverage, i.e. the processes and departments/units covered, and its functionalities, i.e. the nature and extent of the support the IFMIS is expected to provide.						
4	**Commercial Off-the-Shelf Systems (COTS) & Government Information Systems**	To be familiar with Commercial Off-the-Shelf Systems (COTS) which are already being used by governments or which may customized by local government units.						
5	**Accounting and Reporting Applications**	Understanding and using accounting software programs.						
6	**Database Development**	Development and use of databases.						
7	**Requisition Transition**	Use of online requisition process, moving away from manual paper requisitions.						
8	**Funds Availability Transition**	Use of automatic funds verification, and procedures to prevent overspending.						
9	**Forms Transition**	Moving from letters and forms to the use of electronic IDs and approval of transactions.						

10	**Data Entry Transition**	Retiring of the duplicate process of data entry, multiple books, systems, and registers to a database, single entry, format.						
11	**Approval Transition**	Process of using delegated approvals (fewer persons), development of approval hierarchies, establishment of system enforced segregation of responsibilities, management by exceptions; exception reports and alerts.						
12	**The Electronic Audit Trail**	How the electronic audit trail is used, including backup statements of reasons for purchase, scanned documents, and document management.						

6.2 Intermediate - the courses are appropriate for managers with responsibilities related to the administration of a department or projects, programs, or activities related to the topic. Courses are highly interactive and concentrate on the issues/problems of the managers attending the program.

	TRAINING TOPIC	TRAINING OBJECTIVE	RELEVANCE TO WORK 4 – Very Relevant, mandatory for work 3 – Relevant, useful for work 2 – Partially Relevant, some relevance. 1 – Not Relevant, no relation to work				Training Desired	
			4	3	2	1	Yes	No
1	Conceptual Design for Integrated Financial Management Information System (IFMIS)	To recognize the importance of a conceptual Design for IFMIS, to specify objectives of the system, its scope and coverage along with an overview of the PFM Framework, user requirements and key business processes that the system is required to support.						
2	The Shift to a Total Electronic Culture	To identify the specific steps towards the adoption of a Total Electronic Culture: (1) Identification of the Legal Framework for PFM; (2) Functional Analysis of processes and procedures; (3) Synchronization of budget and accounting codes; (4) Capacity Building Requirements; (5) Infrastructure Requirements; (6) Policy / Legislative Support						
3	Interfacing Between Existing Government Information Systems	To develop an integrated IFMIS by linking the existing information systems in the Spending Organization and exploring opportunities for integrating new information systems or Commercial Off-the-Shelf Systems into the existing information systems.						
4	Security of Data Management and Electronic Transactions	To be familiar with control measures which secure and facilitate data management and to identify security measures over the internet, including the use of private-public keys and electronic signatures in electronic mails.						
5	IFMIS Implementation	To identify and apply the steps in IFMIS implementation, drawing lessons from the experience of other countries and Spending Organization in IFMIS implementation.						
6	General Ledger	To identify and utilize IFMIS Software: budget, budget allocations, period structures (months, quarters and financial years), commitments, cash actual, accrual actual).						

7	**Treasury/Cash Management**	To identify and utilize IFMIS Software: recording and reporting cash transactions, linking bank and cash accounts, ceilings for cash accounts, check payment.						
8	**Accounts Payable**	To identify and utilize IFMIS Software: invoice management, receipt of goods, prepayment invoice, advance processing, credit and debit note payment, invoice printing.						
9	**Accounts Receivable**	To identify and utilize IFMIS Software: manage partial payments, refunds for over payment, link to fixed asset management, link to revenue collection (tax and custom).						
10	**Fixed Asset Management**	To identify and utilize IFMIS Software: asset description, location, unique identification, cost and depreciation rate and method.						
11	**Procurement**	To identify and utilize IFMIS Software: requisitions, purchase orders, goods receipting, vendor maintenance, commitment record and validation of funds availability.						
12	**Budget**	To identify and utilize IFMIS Software: budget development, spending limits, relate the budget to the chart of accounts.						
13	**Reporting**	To identify and utilize IFMIS Software: produce financial reports, reporting electronically, printing and exporting reports.						
14	**Interfacing**	To identify and utilize IFMIS Software: linking to: tax collection system, payroll system, debt management system, and bank system.						
15	**Auditing**	To identify and utilize IFMIS Software: supporting the audit trail, recording system log-ins.						

6.3 Advanced - the courses are directed at senior level officials responsible for making policy decisions related to the topic. Courses are highly interactive and may include individual consulting provided to the participants.

	TRAINING TOPIC	TRAINING OBJECTIVE	RELEVANCE TO WORK 4 – Very Relevant, mandatory for work 3 – Relevant, useful for work 2 – Partially Relevant, some relevance. 1 – Not Relevant, no relation to work				Training Desired	
			4	3	2	1	Yes	No
1	**Integrated Financial Management Information System (IFMIS)**	To define the objectives, scope and coverage as well as specific functionalities of IFMIS; and to recognize the benefits of IFMIS versus the risks involved in implementing IFMIS.						
2	**Change Management: Shifting to a Total Electronic Culture**	To identify the change management requirements for shifting to a total electronic culture.						
3	**Transparency and Accountability through IFMIS**	To recognize the impact of IFMIS on corruption and on enhancing public access to information on public resource management.						
4	**Change Management: Preparing for Change**	To use a change management team, conducting the organization assessment, and responsibilities of senior management.						
5	**Change Management: Managing Change**	To develop change plans, executing change plans, and integration into project planning.						
6	**Change Management: Reinforcing Change**	To collect and analyze feedback, diagnose performance gaps, manage resistance, take corrective actions, celebrate successes, plan further improvement.						

7. LEADERSHIP AND GOVERNANCE

7.1 Basic - Courses convey basic learning about the subject. The courses are appropriate for all levels of personnel with an interest to learn more about the topic. Substantial background materials on the subject are distributed.

	TRAINING TOPIC	TRAINING OBJECTIVE	RELEVANCE TO WORK 4 – Very Relevant, mandatory for wor 3 – Relevant, useful for work 2 – Partially Relevant, some relevance. 1 – Not Relevant, no relation to work				Training Desired	
			4	3	2	1	Yes	No
1	**Leadership and Influence**	To define leadership, distinguish it from management, understand the functions of leadership and appreciate the value of shared leadership in an organization.						
2	**Understanding of Spending Organization Public Financial Management**	To gain knowledge about the objectives and main components of Spending Organization PFM.						
3	**Organisation and Staff Management**	To gain an overview of: (1) strategic planning and goal setting; (2) work climate assessment, mission and vision development; (3) organization assessment and redesign; (4) role definition and negotiation; (5) group conflict management; (6) work climate assessment, mission and vision development.						
4	**Human Resource Management**	Basic overview of human resources management, and identification of HRM training needs.						
5	**Team Building Skills**	To use skills to build team morale, cooperation and motivation. Development of a team which is more than a working group. Using coaching skills.						
6	**Delegation of Responsibility and Authority**	To understand and use of the authority to achieve objectives, the responsibility for completing tasks, the accountability for results, and the delegation of responsibilities.						

7	**Work Group Management**	To use techniques for forming groups, identification of individual skills, development of methodologies, assignment of tasks, and establishment of roles.						
8	**Human Behaviour in Organisation**	To understand basic human behaviour and attitudes in organisation and how to interact / adjust to different types of working attitudes.						

7.2 Intermediate - the courses are appropriate for mid-level managers with responsibilities related to the administration of projects, programmes, or activities related to the topic. Courses are highly interactive and concentrate on the issues/problems of the managers attending the program.

	TRAINING TOPIC	TRAINING OBJECTIVE	RELEVANCE TO WORK 4 – Very Relevant, mandatory for work 3 – Relevant, useful for work 2 – Partially Relevant, some relevance. 1 – Not Relevant, no relation to work				Training Desired	
			4	3	2	1	Yes	No
1	**Strategic Planning**	To understand strategic planning, conducting the strategic analysis, setting the strategic direction.						
2	**Setting the Vision & Developing Mission Statements**	To developing the "vision", obtaining buy-in, issues in the vision process, who sets the vision and how? The use of mission statements, development of mission statements, writing quantitative and qualitative performance indicators.						
3	**Making the Budget Match the Vision**	To move from projects to programs, bringing the planning and budgeting cycles closer together, maintaining the focus on the long-term vision.						
4	**Designing and Conducting Efficient and Effective Meetings**	To establish methods to conduct effective meetings, determining the outcome desired, setting the agenda, inviting the right people, gaining participation and commitment, follow-on actions.						
5	**Use of Parliamentary Procedure**	To use of modified parliamentary procedures to organize and run efficient and effective meetings. How to introduce resolutions, the discussion process, amending and changing resolutions, taking comments, voting, assigning tasks.						
6	**Anti-Corruption Measures**	To build anti-corruption attitudes, preparing systems to prevent corruption, obtaining high level support.						
7	**Bribery, Extortion, Nepotism and Patronage**	To protect yourself from corrupt behaviors. Using methods of transparency which protect you from advances by corrupt individuals.						

7.3 Advanced - the courses are directed at government officials responsible for making policy and high-level management decisions related to the topic. Courses are highly interactive and may include individual consulting provided to the participants.

	TRAINING TOPIC	TRAINING OBJECTIVE	RELEVANCE TO WORK 4 – Very Relevant, mandatory for work 3 – Relevant, useful for work 2 – Partially Relevant, some relevance. 1 – Not Relevant, no relation to work				Training Desired	
			4	3	2	1	Yes	No
1	Change Management and Leadership	To introduce a programme of change into a ministry, department or unit. Utilising leadership skills to develop and implement a programme of change.						
2	Public Policy for Leadership	To understand the role of leadership in the development of public policy, understanding the role of the public in the development of public policy, moving from concepts - from leadership policy to management administration.						
3	Legal Framework for Spending Organisation Public Financial Management System	To understand laws and regulations which are involved in public financial management issues.						
4	Championing the Mandate	To being personally committed to and taking initiatives to promote and enhance the mission and mandate of the institution						
5	Responsibility for societal impact	To effectively manage the relationships and boundaries between the institution and the larger society						
6.	Empowering Delivery	To drive for excellence by providing transparency and openness about performance, goals, standards and measures. Giving ongoing objective feedback against clear standards						
7	Building Sustainability	To build systems, structure, and capability of the institution to ensure sustainable delivery of predictable results.						
8	Leveraging Diversity	To recognize and leverage relevant aspects of difference (race, gender, other sensitivities) as relating to organisational performance that enhances the effectiveness of the institution.						
9	Developing Others	To develop the technical skills and leadership abilities of all personnel, not just direct reports, to create sustainable delivery capability						

10	**Conceptual Thinking**	To assimilate and apply new information, principles, best practices or past experiences in a useful way to support the objectives of the institution. Making the complex understandable and actionable to others						
11	**Understanding Aspects of the Changing External Environment**	To develop a forward view around areas, such as, models of service, increasing public expectations, funding constraints and capacity building						
12	**Knowledge and Understanding**	To develop knowledge and understanding of programmes that actively promote aid effectiveness, poverty reduction, environmental issues, social discrimination and exclusion, anti-corruption, and human rights						
13	**Anti-corruption Policy**	To gain knowledge and understanding of anti-corruption policy and economic crimes, such as, bribery, abuse of office, fraud, extortion, favouritism, mis-appropriation of public funds, breach of trust, grapping of public property, conflict of interest, bid rigging, failure to pay taxes, fees or charges to a public body and to develop structures to prevent, detect, investigate, report and deal with corruption						

8. MANAGEMENT

8.1 Basic - the courses convey basic learning about the subject. These are appropriate for all levels of personnel with an interest to learn more about the topic. Substantial background materials on the subject are distributed.

	TRAINING TOPIC	TRAINING OBJECTIVE	RELEVANCE TO WORK 4 – Very Relevant, mandatory for work 3 – Relevant, useful for work 2 – Partially Relevant, some relevance. 1 – Not Relevant, no relation to work				Training Desired	
			4	3	2	1	Yes	No
1	**The Local Government Structure and Public Financial Management**	To understand the structures of the local government, how they interrelate, and how public financial management tasks are carried out in the organization.						
2	**Project Management**	To understand the phases of a project, the tools and techniques for managing a project and standards for project management.						
3	**Supervisory Management**	To learn how to make the shift to being a supervisor, planning and organizing, and dealing with staff, including motivation, work allocation and delegation.						
4	**Time Management**	To develop ability to successfully manage time and focus on high priority tasks. To learn proper prioritization of tasks and to handle bad time keeping situations.						

8.2 Intermediate - the courses are appropriate for mid-level managers with responsibilities related to the administration of projects, programs, or activities related to the topic. Courses are highly interactive and concentrate on the issues/problems of the managers attending the program.

TRAINING TOPIC		TRAINING OBJECTIVE	RELEVANCE TO WORK 4 – Very Relevant, mandatory for work 3 – Relevant, useful for work 2 – Partially Relevant, some relevance. 1 – Not Relevant, no relation to work				Training Desired	
			4	3	2	1	Yes	No
1	The New Manager Training	To move into being a manager, understand the importance of the manager's role manager, deal with difficult people and conflicts, and effectively communicate with team members.						
2	Programme Analysis and Work and Financial Plan Development	To develop programs and Work & Financial Plans which ensure the delivery of public goods and services to the Spending Organization's constituents.						
3	Performance Reviews and Results Management	To conduct performance reviews based on the approved budget and physical and financial performance targets. To analyze results, institute corresponding measures, and monitor and control implementation of measures.						
4	Adjustment Proposals	To incorporate changes in program expenditures and adjust plans according to the results of the periodic budget performance review.						
5	Organization and Staffing	To review the organization and staffing pattern and developing a lean but more efficient and effective organizational structure and staffing pattern.						
6	Transparency and Public Access to Documents	To effectively manage public records, increase and promote public access to documents related to financial transactions, and to develop a list of exceptions for data which should not be publicly shared pursuant to existing laws, rules and regulations.						
7	Conflict Management Training	To identify factors causing conflict, understand basic types of behavior and how to adjust to each type for conflict prevention, evaluate the situation and implement viable solutions to the conflict.						

8	**Report Preparation and Communication**	To develop of skills in the preparation of reports and the communication of key findings, and recommendations.						
9	**Revenue and Expenditure Reports Analysis**	To analyze revenue reports. Ensuring that budget appropriations are available and utilized as planned.						
10	**Cash Flow Reports Preparation and Analysis**	To develop and use cash flow reports. How to shorten the cash flow cycle and minimize the available cash.						
11	**Mid-Term Budget Performance Reviews**	To Conduct a mid-term physical and financial performance review based on the Annual Budget and Physical & Financial Performance Targets.						
12	**Adjustment Proposals**	To incorporate changes in program expenditures and adjust plans according to the results of the mid-term budget performance review.						
13	**Organisation and Staffing**	To review the organization and staffing pattern and developing a lean but more efficient and effective organizational structure and staffing pattern.						

8.3 Advanced - the courses are directed at local government officials responsible for making policy and high-level management decisions related to the topic. Courses are highly interactive and may include individual consulting provided to the participants.

	TRAINING TOPIC	TRAINING OBJECTIVE	RELEVANCE TO WORK 4 – Very Relevant, mandatory for work 3 – Relevant, useful for work 2 – Partially Relevant, some relevance. 1 – Not Relevant, no relation to work				Training Desired	
			4	3	2	1	Yes	No
1	**Public Financial Management**	To understand the objectives, components and structures of Public Financial Management and formulate policy in support of Spending Organization PFM Improvement.						
2	**Management of the Financial Team**	Define and differentiate the roles of the members of the Local Finance Committee / PFM Team and establish systems and procedures which will allow the team to assume a more active managerial role in PFM.						
3	**Organisation and Staffing Management**	To learn how to review the organization and staffing pattern and develop a rationalized but more efficient and effective organizational structure and staffing pattern. To formulate policies which provide for Capacity Building at the organization and individual levels.						
4	**Public Financial Management Assessment**	To understand and effectively administer the PFM Assessment Tool (PFMAT), and analyze and utilize results for policy decisions.						

9. PLANNING, MONITORING AND EVALUATION

9.1 Basic - the courses convey basic learning about the subject. Courses are appropriate for all levels of personnel with an interest to learn more about the topic. Substantial background materials on the subject are distributed.

	TRAINING TOPIC	TRAINING OBJECTIVE	RELEVANCE TO WORK 4 – Very Relevant, mandatory for work 3 – Relevant, useful for work 2 – Partially Relevant, some relevance. 1 – Not Relevant, no relation to work				Training Desired	
			4	3	2	1	Yes	No
1	**Introduction to Project Management**	To define a project, identify the project cycle, and understand the project cycle management concept, including the steps for successfully managing a project.						
2	**Basic Course on Project Planning**	To recognize the importance of project planning, identify the steps and tools for planning simple and complex projects.						
3	**Project Control**	To define project control, recognize the importance of project control mechanisms and identify the tools for managing variances in planned items and anticipated changes and risks in the project.						
4	**Project Performance Monitoring and Evaluation**	To understand the basic terminologies and concepts of project evaluation and learn how to apply project monitoring and evaluation approaches and techniques.						
5	**Overview of the Project Management Toolbox**	To be familiar with all the tools and techniques for project management and to identify when and where to use these tools and techniques.						

9.2 Intermediate - the courses are appropriate for managers with responsibilities related to the administration of a department or projects, programs, or activities related to the topic. Courses are highly interactive and concentrate on the issues/problems of the managers attending the program.

	TRAINING TOPIC	TRAINING OBJECTIVE	RELEVANCE TO WORK 4 – Very Relevant, mandatory for work 3 – Relevant, useful for work 2 – Partially Relevant, some relevance. 1 – Not Relevant, no relation to work				Training Desired	
			4	3	2	1	Yes	No
1	**Advanced Course on Project Management**	To define a project and identify the project lifecycle, understand the concept of project management, and learn how to use essential management tools in managing and monitoring the project within the wider context of social and environmental issues, finance, organization, procurement and people management.						
2	**Project Time Estimation and Scheduling**	To recognize the importance of accurate time estimation and apply tools / techniques for determining time requirements for specific tasks and building a schedule for simple projects.						
3	**Project Risk Management**	To define project risk management, recognize the importance of detecting and addressing risks, and to learn how to use tools / techniques for managing risks *(e.g. Risk Impact/Probability Chart)*.						
4	**Project Planning & Scheduling for Complex Projects**	To understand the project planning framework and process and apply various tools for project planning: (1) GANTT Chart; and (2)PERT-CPM.						
5	**Project Planning Using the Logical Framework Approach**	To understand the project planning framework and process, and apply the Logical Framework Approach and develop project log frames.						
6	**Project Performance Monitoring and Evaluation**	To (1) distinguish between monitoring and evaluation; (2) to apply the logical framework approach in designing and evaluating projects; (3) to learn how to formulate performance indicators; (4) collect and analyze data; and (5) communicate results.						

7	The Organisational Performance Indicator Framework (OPIF) and Logical Framework Formulation	To understand the concept and value of the Organisational Performance Indicator Framework (OPIF), and to formulate an OPIF logical framework for the Spending Organization, Department and Unit.						

9.3 Advanced - the courses are directed at senior level officials responsible for making policy decisions related to the topic. Courses are highly interactive and may include individual consulting provided to the participants.

	TRAINING TOPIC	TRAINING OBJECTIVE	RELEVANCE TO WORK 4 – Very Relevant, mandatory for work 3 – Relevant, useful for work 2 – Partially Relevant, some relevance. 1 – Not Relevant, no relation to work				Training Desired	
			4	3	2	1	Yes	No
1	**Advanced Course on Project Management**	To define a project and identify the project lifecycle, understand the concept of project management, and learn how to use essential management tools in managing and monitoring the project, with emphasis on the environment within which the project management process is carried out.						
2	**Stakeholder Analysis and Planning**	To recognize the benefits of using a stakeholder-based approach in project management; and to identify tools for identifying and prioritizing stakeholders and gaining support for the project.						
3	**The Organisational Performance Indicator Framework (OPIF) and Logical Framework Formulation**	To understand the concept and value of the Organizational Performance Indicator Framework (OPIF), and to formulate an OPIF logical framework for the Spending Organization, Department and Unit.						
4	**Strategic Risks Management**	To understand all aspects of risks, including, level of impact, areas of risk, risk description (cause and consequence), mitigation / control,						

10. PROCUREMENT

10.1 Basic - the courses convey basic learning about the subject. The course is appropriate for all levels of personnel with an interest to learn more about the topic. Substantial background materials on the subject are distributed.

	TRAINING TOPIC	TRAINING OBJECTIVE	RELEVANCE TO WORK 4 – Very Relevant, mandatory for work 3 – Relevant, useful for work 2 – Partially Relevant, some relevance. 1 – Not Relevant, no relation to work				Training Desired	
			4	3	2	1	Yes	No
1	**Business process design**	Understand the current design of procurement steps.						
2	**Public Procurement Management**	Overview of the functions of public procurement management, including; bidding and negotiating process, handling of acquired goods, transferring management control and liability, and contracts.						
3	**Procurement for Externally Financed Projects**	Understanding of externally financed projects. Use of appropriate procurement models.						
4	**The Government Procurement Act)**	To identify the basic principles, scope and coverage of the general principles governing procurement organizations and procurement planning.						
5	**Preparing and Updating Project Procurement and Management Plans and Annual Procurement Plans**	To apply the general principles of procurement planning and facilitate the formulation of realistic and reliable procurement plans that can serve as monitoring and evaluation tools as well.						
6	**Standard Bidding Procedures and Alternative Modes for the Procurement of Goods and Services, Civil Works and Consulting Services**	To identify and apply the standard bidding procedures and alternative modes for the procurement of goods and services, civil works and consulting services.						
7	**Documents (PBDs)**	To identify the contents of the Bidding Documents and facilitate their preparation and use during the Spending Organization's procurement activities.						

8	**Ethics in Procurement**	To recognise the need to keep ethics at the forefront of all procurement activities and be familiarized with the criminal, civil and administrative liabilities involved in government procurement.						
9	**Contract Implementation**	To identify post contract award activities, including the issuance of Amendments to Orders / Variation Orders, Advance Payments, Suspension of Work, Liquidated Damages and Warranties.						

10.2 Intermediate - the courses are appropriate for mid-level managers with responsibilities related to the administration of projects, programs, or activities related to the topic. Courses are highly interactive and concentrate on the issues/problems of the managers attending the program.

	TRAINING TOPIC	TRAINING OBJECTIVE	RELEVANCE TO WORK 4 – Very Relevant, mandatory for work 3 – Relevant, useful for work 2 – Partially Relevant, some relevance. 1 – Not Relevant, no relation to work				Training Desired	
			4	3	2	1	Yes	No
1	Government Procurement and its Implementing Rules	To identify the basic principles, scope and coverage of the general principles governing procurement organizations and procurement planning.						
2	Preparing and Updating Project Procurement and Management Plans and Annual Procurement Plans	To apply the general principles of procurement planning and facilitate the formulation of realistic and reliable procurement plans that can serve as monitoring and evaluation tools as well.						
3	Price Monitoring of Goods and Services	To recognize the importance of maintaining a price monitoring system and be familiar with National Government Agencies which could provide information and technical support in establishing a price monitoring system in the Spending Organization.						
4	Maintenance of Registry of Suppliers and Contractors	To facilitate the establishment and maintenance of a manual or electronic registry of suppliers and contractors, using as take off points the experience of National Government Agencies with a functional registry of suppliers/contractors.						
5	Ethics in Procurement	To recognize the need to keep ethics at the forefront of all procurement activities and be familiarized with the criminal, civil and administrative liabilities involved in government procurement.						
6	Contract Implementation	To identify post contract award activities, including the issuance of Amendments to Orders / Variation Orders, Advance Payments, Suspension of Work, Liquidated Damages and Warranties.						
7	Moving Toward IT Procurement	Coordination with FMIS and ICT to ensure that procurements meet special requirements for use of electronic bidding and documentation.						

8	**Public and Private Partnership (PPP), and Build-Operate-Transfer (BOT)**	Understanding and use of PPP and BOT methodologies in the procurement of major works in collaboration with the private sector.							
9	**Vendor Rating and Performance Review**	Maintaining a database of vendors, including those which are "black listed" from government procurement.							
10	**The principles of stock management**	Overview of the functions of stock management, receiving, storage, rotation, and delivery to end user.							
11	**Standard Bidding Document (SBD)**	Understanding and utilizing SBDs: world bank, ADB, EU model. SBDs for RFPs, RFQs, Procurement for Works, Procurement of Consulting Service, and Procurement for Health Sector Goods.							
12	**Developing Spending Organisation-specific Procurement Manuals**	To facilitate the review of the Spending Organization's existing procurement procedures and to develop Spending Organisation-specific procurement manuals.							

10.3 Advanced - the courses are directed at local government officials responsible for making policy and high-level management decisions related to the topic. Courses are highly interactive and may include individual consulting provided to the participants.

	TRAINING TOPIC	TRAINING OBJECTIVE	RELEVANCE TO WORK 4 – Very Relevant, mandatory for work 3 – Relevant, useful for work 2 – Partially Relevant, some relevance. 1 – Not Relevant, no relation to work				Training Desired	
			4	3	2	1	Yes	No
1	**The Government Procurement and its Implementing Rules and Regulations**	To identify the basic principles, scope and coverage of Various Acts, including the general principles governing procurement organisations and procurement planning.						
2	**Procurement Organisations and Benefits and Indemnification Packages**	To be familiarized with the procurement organization, the respective roles, duties and functions of the members of the procurement organisation and the benefits and indemnification packages due.						
3	**Procurement Planning and the Planning-Budgeting Cycle in Spending Organizations**	To recognize the importance and procedures of procurement planning and its integration in the Planning-Budgeting Cycle of Spending Organizations.						
4	**Blacklisting Procedures**	To be familiarized with the guidelines and procedures for blacklisting of suppliers and contractors.						
5	**Resolving Protests and Other Disputes Arising from Bidding Procedures and Contract Implementation**	To identify and apply the Rules on Protest and Dispute Resolution following applicable laws, rules and regulations.						
6	**Ethics in Procurement**	To recognise the need to keep ethics at the forefront of all procurement activities and be familiarised with the criminal, civil and administrative liabilities involved in government procurement.						

11. PROFESSIONAL DEVELOPMENT

11.1 Basic - the courses convey basic learning about the subject. The courses are appropriate for all levels of personnel with an interest to learn more about the topic. Substantial background materials on the subject are distributed.

	TRAINING TOPIC	TRAINING OBJECTIVE	RELEVANCE TO WORK 4 – Very Relevant, mandatory for work 3 – Relevant, useful for work 2 – Partially Relevant, some relevance. 1 – Not Relevant, no relation to work				Training Desired	
			4	3	2	1	Yes	No
1	**Foundation Skills** (*Learning How to Learn*)	To understand and utilize efficient learning strategies, hence, absorb and apply training more quickly; to distinguish between essential and non-essential information, discern patterns in information and identify the actions necessary to improve job performance.						
2	**Communication Skills (Oral and Listening)**	To develop skills in expressing ideas orally and improve the ability to take and understand instructions, to improve presentation skills, and develop the ability to give clients as well as supervisors feedback.						
3	**Career Development Skills**	To develop the ability to actively manage work life in a rapidly changing environment, including stress management.						
4	**Relating to Others and Developing Interpersonal Skills**	To recognize and improve the ability to determine appropriate self-behavior, particularly in the workplace, cope with undesirable behavior in others, absorb stress, deal with ambiguity, structure social interaction, share responsibility, and interact more easily with others.						
5	**Technical Writing Skills**	To develop the ability to write project proposals by understanding the proposal writing process, proposal audience, and proposal writing practices. To learn how to prepare technical reports, including report outlining, research, drafting, documentation, and relating the report to the TOR.						

6	**Effective Public Speaking**	To understand the fundamentals of effective speaking, learn how to make prepared and impromptu speeches and develop techniques in delivering speeches / talks.						
7	**Stress Management**	To learn how to cope with and manage stress in the work environment.						

11.2 Intermediate - the courses are appropriate for managers with responsibilities related to the administration of a department or projects, programs, or activities related to the topic. Courses are highly interactive and concentrate on the issues/problems of the managers attending the program.

	TRAINING TOPIC	TRAINING OBJECTIVE	RELEVANCE TO WORK 4 – Very Relevant, mandatory for work 3 – Relevant, useful for work 2 – Partially Relevant, some relevance. 1 – Not Relevant, no relation to work				Training Desired	
			4	3	2	1	Yes	No
1	**Training of Trainers**	To learn methodologies of professional training, including how to lead sessions, involve participants and provide coaching.						
2	**Session Plan Development**	To develop sessions, work with resource experts, and utilize the 3 steps in session design.						
3	**Effective Course Design**	To develop skills in identifying course content and development of applications.						
4	**Trainings for Professional Accreditation**	To obtain Continuing Professional Education (CPE) Units required for professional accreditation *(depends on the Profession)*.						
5	**Human Resource Management**	To understand the principles and components of human resources management, and identification of HRM training needs.						
6	**Capacity Building Program Preparation**	To learn how to conduct a Training Needs Analysis and utilize results in preparing a Capacity Building Program for the Spending Organization.						
7	**Stress Management**	To learn how to cope with and manage stress in the work environment.						

11.3 Advanced - the courses are directed at senior level officials responsible for making policy decisions related to the topic. Courses are highly interactive and may include individual consulting provided to the participants.

	TRAINING TOPIC	TRAINING OBJECTIVE	RELEVANCE TO WORK 4 – Very Relevant, mandatory for work 3 – Relevant, useful for work 2 – Partially Relevant, some relevance. 1 – Not Relevant, no relation to work				Training Desired	
			4	3	2	1	Yes	No
1	**Developing Policy Support for Capacity Building Programs**	To understand the importance of a Capacity Building Program for the organization and individual employee and to formulate policy support for continuing capability building in the Spending Organization.						
2	**Professional Membership and Accreditation**	To understand the importance of participating in professional organizations, and establishment of policy support for the professionalization and accreditation of the Spending Organization, and its officials and employees.						
3	**Budgeting for Capacity building Programmes**	To understand the need for strengthened budget support for capacity building; to learn how to establish a realistic and responsive budget for capacity building programs; and to identify different implementation schemes, including procurement modes.						
4	**Importance of Employee Capacity Enhancement in the Attainment of Organisational Objectives**	To assess the need to develop and enhance the technical employees and the value of capacity building in the attainment of organizational goals and objectives. To develop policies and guidelines in the prioritization of the conduct of capacity enhancement.						
5	**Training / Review for Management Aptitude Test Battery (MATB) Examinations and Assessment Center Exams**	To prepare for the Management Aptitude Test Battery Examinations conducted by the Career Executive Service Board.						

REFERENCES

1. Committee of Public Accounts Transforming contract management Twenty-third report of Session 2014-15 HC 585 10 December 2014
2. National Audit Office Report, Cabinet Office, Transforming government's contract management, para 3.17. HC 269 Session 2013-14, 4 September 2014
3. Provision of Training Services on Public Finance Management and Procurement for Government of South Sudan launched under CBTF 2.August 2010
4. Civil Service Regulations, Ministry of Labour, Public Service and Human Resources Development, GoSS, February, 2007;
5. Framework on Human Resource Management Policy, Strategy and Plan, J.Emerson Jones (2003)
6. Competency Development Framework, J.Emerson Jones (June, 2004);

Selected Worldwide Web Sites

https://www.gov.uk/government/publications/ tone-from-the-top -leadership-ethics-andaccountability-in-policing

http://www.pwc.com/gx/en/ethics-businessconduct/code-of-conduct. jhtml

http://www. pwc.com/gx/en/ethics-business-conduct/ethics-questions. jhtml

https://www.cips.org/en-GB/training-courses/ Ethical-Procurement -and-Supply-/

https://www.instituteforgovernment.org.uk/blog/delivering-development-lessonsdfid%E2%80%99s-implementation-units.

www.ingramcontent.com/pod-product-compliance
Lightning Source LLC
Chambersburg PA
CBHW050431290526
45786CB00003B/1487